Sometimes my face is happy.

Sometimes my face is sad.

Sometimes my face is worried.

Sometimes my face is mad.

Sometimes I have a proud face.

Sometimes my face looks hurt.

Sometimes my face is hard to read, caked with grime and dirt.

Sometimes I wear my brave face.

Sometimes my face looks blue.

Sometimes it is confused if I am
not sure what to do.

Sometimes my face looks guilty;
you can see it in my eyes.

Sometimes my face looks
shocked, filled with pure surprise.

Sometimes my face looks bored.

Sometimes it is full of zest.

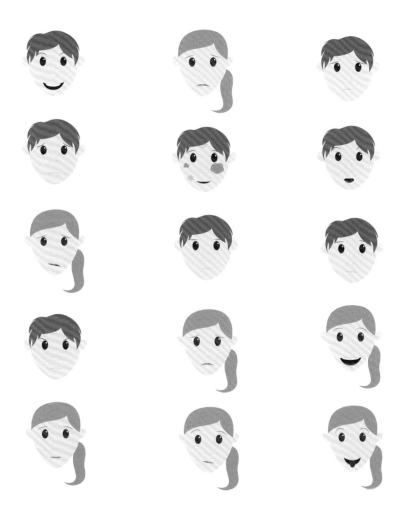

I have a lot of faces.

I like my funny face the best.

Activities

Talk about what these images are telling you about the story.

Activities

Talk about what these images are telling you about the story.

Activities

Talk about what these images are telling you about the story.

Activities

Talk about what these images are telling you about the story.